MW00908941

LIBRA

LIBRA

Let your Sun sign show you the way
to a happy and fulfilling life

Marion Williamson & Pam Carruthers

ARCTURUS

This edition published in 2021 by Arcturus Publishing
Limited
26/27 Bickels Yard, 151–153 Bermondsey Street,
London SE1 3HA

ISBN: 978-1-83940-145-9
AD008764UK

Printed in China

CONTENTS

Introduction

*W*elcome, Libra! You have just taken a step towards what might become a lifelong passion. When astrology gets under your skin, there's no going back. Astrology helps you understand yourself and the people around you, and its dazzling insights become more fascinating the deeper you go.

Just as the first humans turned to the life-giving Sun for sustenance and guidance, your astrological journey begins with your Sun sign of Libra. First we delve deeply into the heart of what makes you tick, then we'll continue to unlock your cosmic potential by exploring love, your career and health, where you might prefer to live, and how you get along with family and friends.

Then it's over to gifted astrologer, Pam Carruthers, for her phenomenal birthdate analysis, where she gives personality insights for your specific Libra birthday.

In the last part of the book we get right inside how astrology works by revealing the different layers that will help you understand your own birth chart, and offer the planetary tools to get you started.

Are you ready, Libra? Let's weigh up the finer points of your balanced personality ...

CUSP DATES FOR LIBRA
24 September – 23 October

The exact time of the Sun's entry into each zodiac sign varies every year, so it's impossible to list them all. If you were born a day either side of the dates above, you're a 'cusp' baby. This means you may feel like you're a blend of Libra/Virgo or Libra/Scorpio, or you may instinctively just know that you're one sign right to your core.

Going deeper

If you want to know once and for all whether you're a Virgo, Libra or Scorpio, you can look up your birthdate in a planetary ephemeris, of which there are plenty online. (See page 102 for more information.) This shows the exact moment the Sun moved into a new zodiac sign for the month you were born.

The Libra personality

*Y*ou are an intellectual Air sign ruled by romantic, charming, Venus. As an Air sign you are one of the zodiac's thinkers and communicators, and with relationship-oriented Venus as your ruler, you crave harmonious rapport, balance and fairness with everyone you encounter. You are one of the most sociable signs of the zodiac, and your desire to please others and dislike of conflict, means you sometimes sacrifice your own ambitions to keep the peace. Your astrological symbol is the Scales, representing your fair judgment, excellent taste and love of symmetry. Because you are so concerned with making the right decisions it can take you a long time to weigh up all the options, but when you have made up your mind, it's usually set in stone … unless too many people disagree with you, in which case you may have to rethink!

THE QUEST FOR LOVE

As the seventh of the 12 zodiac signs, you are the first to have an opposite number, and your longing for a partner is one of your strongest motivations. You were born to share, discuss and consider your thoughts and feelings with others, and you need strong relationships to make you feel more complete. It's natural for you to ponder others' opinions before you make up your own mind – even if you don't necessarily agree with them. Bouncing ideas back against someone else somehow makes your own thoughts feel more solid and real. You find it easier to see yourself through the eyes of other people, and so their good opinion seems essential if you are to have good opinion of yourself.

Ruled by affectionate, amorous Venus, romantic love is one of your highest priorities. You are usually either in love or pursuing a new romance. And your relationship with your other half will usually dominate your thoughts. As a mentally-focussed Air sign, you are in love with the *idea* of love – yearning for another, the uniting of soulmates, and the wonder of romantic possibilities. Sex is, of course, a beautiful part of the deal but the physical aspects of love aren't usually as important to you than the companionship, friendliness and sharing.

If you have preponderance of independent Fire signs in your birth chart you may not be as dependent on others for your happiness, as a true Libra often is. It's important that you spend some of your time living alone, so that you learn you can be truly happy without a significant other. It's all too easy for you to feel bonded to others' opinions, likes and fears, but the answers to what you want from life can only come from deep within you.

To help you discover who you really are, you may, quite unconsciously, see others as a mirror. This can sometimes mean you remain with a partner for far too long, hoping that either things will improve, or just out of the fear of being alone. However, when you let yourself explore different types or relationships with a variety of people, you will discover how you differ from them, and what makes you unique. It's often a balancing act between you and others, and your thoughts and emotions. But weighing things up is what you were born to do!

BEAUTY IN ALL THINGS

Both Taurus and Libra are Venus-ruled and have a deep appreciation for beauty and the finer things in life. Taurus is an Earth sign, so their love tends to be expressed through a desire for tangible things, such as food, comfort and money. In Air sign Libra, your Venusian sensibilities are conveyed though the expression of ideas – intellectual compatibility, wit, excellent manners, refined tastes, intelligence and appearance. You can be quite particular about how you decorate and beautify your environment – and yourself!

You may refuse to answer the door if you think you're looking shabby. Even in a hospital bed you'll be the cute one with shiny hair, stylish pyjamas, designer stubble or full make-up. You dress well and are a dedicated follower of fashion, enjoying colour, eye-catching designs and sumptuous fabrics. Style usually trumps comfort in your eyes, and you'll plump for gorgeous shoes over uglier, more practical varieties every time. Your luxury-loving Venusian tastes often stretch your budget but you'll gladly go into the red for a beautiful bit of tailoring. You have an outfit for every occasion and you always notice what other people are wearing.

Your environment needs to reflect your refined tastes, too, and your home will be a clutter-free, peaceful space, artfully decorated and aesthetically pleasing. Fresh flowers, candles and some contemporary works of art will adorn your perfectly painted walls.

CHAMPAGNE TASTE, PAUPER'S BUDGET?

Venus is the planet most associated with money, but where the other Venus sign, Taurus, tends to save carefully and sensibly, you're in awe of all the luxurious and enjoyable items that money allows you to experience – that's what you think credit cards are for! You rival extravagant Leo as one the zodiac's most lavish spenders and if you have enough in the black, you see it as money to be spent rather than saved or invested.

You live for your social life and, when you have it, you lend and spend on your friends so that everyone else can enjoy the good times with you. Amazing holidays, gorgeous clothes and fine dining all feature prominently in your spending habits. You see money as the way to make your life more exciting and glamorous now, rather than waiting to be able to afford enjoyable new things. You love quality and style but you're not a rash spender, frittering away small amounts or living in denial of your bank balance. You're perfectly clear about where it all goes – and you enjoy every penny!

TO BE FAIR

As you are the sign of balance and the zodiac's diplomat, you insist you hear all sides of a story before deciding what the fairest course of action should be. An excellent listener, you empathise with everyone's account and don't take immediate action before you have considered all options. You try to be as impartial as possible, which wins you many friends and you always know all the gossip, because the people around you genuinely value your judgment and share all the juicy details.

Your instinctive peace-making skills do sometimes come at a price though, as constantly seeing things from other peoples' points of view can obscure your own feelings and be at the expense of your own swift and dynamic decision-making. People-pleasing is such second nature to you that you lose sight of your own power to decide where to go, and with whom. Your exceptional tolerance can sometimes lead others to take advantage of your good nature or they might assume you will always back them up. Often fearing to rock the boat too much, less scrupulous individuals can become frustrated with your passivity, and can goad you into making decisions that you're not quite ready for.

Always giving people the benefit of the doubt is an admirable personality trait, as long as you are dealing with people who have equally high morals. At some point in your life you may find yourself in a far from perfect relationship or situation, where you have continued uncomplaining and forgiving for months or years. On an unconscious level you may have been registering that things are not working, but the scales haven't quite tipped one way or the other. Then, quite out of the blue, after a small disagreement, you suddenly tip – your mind is made up and there's no going back.

ARIES LESSON

Opposite signs of the zodiac reflect particular areas of our personality that we have not explored or fully developed. Usually they share many similarities but it's where they differ that compels the opposite signs together. Your opposite sign is fiery, Mars-ruled Aries. You're both terrified and in awe of Aries. They say exactly what's on their mind, apparently without fear of offending anyone, and yet other people seem charmed by their boldness and honesty. It's your grace and politeness that usually prevents you from being too honest or saying exactly what's on your mind, and your reverence for social niceties holds your tongue. You're a little scared to stick to your guns as ruthlessly as brutally as decisive Aries, in case you're not taking the whole picture into account or being unfair. But you secretly admire Aries self-sufficiency and openness. You teach Aries that to get what you want takes more than courage, discernment and cooperation are also required. In turn, Aries's lesson for you is to stand on your own two feet and to be your authentic self without apology.

Libra Motto

THE BEST PERSON
TO TALK TO ABOUT
YOUR RELATIONSHIP
IS THE PERSON
YOU'RE IN THE
RELATIONSHIP WITH.

Libra in love

*Y*ou're an old-fashioned romantic Libra, and you want the whole fairytale! You're an intellectual Air sign ruled by Venus, the love and relationship planet, so searching for romantic fulfilment is a crucial part of your existence. Libra is the sign of partnership, of looking at the world from outside of oneself, and a true Libra will long to meet their soulmate.

You love the drama and ceremony of romance, and you absolutely expect to find it. Though, because this is such an important aspect of your life, you may take an inordinately long time to make up your mind about exactly what you're looking for in a life partner. It's just too important a decision to be made lightly.

FLIRTY AND CHARMING

Your attractive, sociable personality and comely smile ensure you won't be short of admirers. If someone takes your fancy, you'll weigh up the pros and cons before finding out more about him or her. You take great pleasure in the more genteel aspects of courtship, but you can be extremely seductive when you're attracted to someone – and very hard to resist!

Your intended will be able to keep you entertained with their wit, and as a loquacious Air sign you get a kick out of sending flirty messages back and forth. A potential partner has to appeal to you mentally, perhaps even as something of a fantasy figure, before you'll up your game.

Going on romantic dates, sending each other thoughtful gifts and letting yourself be chased and wooed, are all thrilling stages of true love for you. The excitement of the initial swoony passion of a new love affair, where you both crash into lamp posts daydreaming of the other, is your rose-tinted Libra idea of heaven. Once you've weighed up all the possibilities and decided to go for it, you shower your other half with love and attention. You are thoughtful and affectionate and always thinking up ways to please the one you adore.

EQUALITY AND SHARING

Disliking chaos, discord and negativity, you are very sensitive to any of your partner's criticisms and you worry about what they really think. It's important for you both to be able to talk candidly at the start of a relationship and to pledge always to communicate. You need reassurance that everything is going well, and you can become resentful if you're on the end of any silent treatment without knowing precisely why. You must feel that you're an equal partner and are not solely responsible for your beloved's good – or bad – moods.

Togetherness is your favourite thing and snuggling up on the sofa with your other half for a lazy night in is one of your favourite things, as long as there's good quality nibbles, wine, and an arty film in the offing. But you also love showing your lover off. You're a sociable type who enjoys dressing up to be seen in the hottest places and you'll want to share the glam high life with your chosen companion.

TRICKY EMOTIONS

You feel deeply unsettled by angry scenes, chaos and noise, so shy away from conflict or arguments. If your partner says something harsh, or if they're loud and angry you find it really difficult to respond. Arguments and ugly scenes have you running for the hills. Your politeness prevents you from being outspoken, even when you feel you ought to be sticking up for yourself. It feels so uncomfortable when your sense of harmony is disrupted that you'll make the peace as quickly as possible – even if you're not the person in the wrong.

Your fear of confrontation can occasionally be used against you by less scrupulous types, and not being able to voice your anger can make you feel powerless. Being completely honest with your lover is a challenge, not only because of the unbearable tension, but because of your indecisiveness and unwillingness to take any action.

Telling others exactly where you stand is probably a skill you'll learn from experience. But life will get easier once you realise that the sky doesn't fall down if you voice an opinion, and others will respect you for being honest.

Most compatible
love signs

Gemini – the good-natured banter you share will keep you both in stitches and you'll always be able to surprise each other.

Aquarius – sociable Aquarius enjoys your wit and charm and learns from your people-pleasing skills, while you learn how to be less concerned about what others think.

Leo – you're a two-person party! You both love the limelight and being seen at your best, but you can laze about in style together, too.

Least compatible
love signs

Cancer – you have some trouble understanding each other's emotions as your feelings propel you towards people while Cancer's make them scuttle away.

Capricorn – solemn Capricorns make you laugh with their dry sense of humour but they're naturally reserved and haughty where you're effusive and open.

Virgo – you get on well as friends, as you both appreciate excellent craftsmanship and notice details others miss, but Virgo's a realist and you're a romantic.

Libra at work

*B*ehind your sweet, sociable personality, lies a shrewd business brain. As one of the zodiac's most skilled communicators you understand how to persuade people to work together, and you're one of the few signs of the zodiac who really knows how to delegate. Well-liked in the work-place, you go out of your way to please your co-workers and easily make friends at the office. Colleagues know you to be a friendly, chilled and witty character, and you're actually surprisingly cool and logical when faced with stressful or complicated tasks. Sharp, clever and creative, you are as good at knitting the details together as you are at spotting errors.

Seeking balance in all things, you're neither a workaholic, or lazy, and seek to level your industriousness fervour with after-work drinks, laughter and cake. Your office or desk is usually the most fun place for your co-workers to hang out, and your love of sharing extends to sharing salacious gossip. You're happy to assist co-workers who need a helping hand and will listen patiently to their woes with a sympathetic ear. You form lifelong friends in the workplace – from the office junior to the CEO, and you treat everyone with the same easy respect and cordial good humour.

MAKING A BEAUTIFUL WORLD

Your Venusian ruler compels you to create a more harmonious and beautiful world. Artistic and creative, you have an affinity with good design that's user friendly, and you might enjoy building sleek websites or working as a graphic designer. Your eye for colour and desire for pleasant surroundings might spur you on to become an interior designer or architect, and many Libra work in the music and fashion industries. The beauty industry may appeal too, especially if combined with more social aspects of the job. Life as a make-up artist, costume designer, hairdresser or masseuse, should be enjoyable as you could combine your social and artistic abilities. Your celebrated interpersonal skills open up public relations as an option, and resolving conflicts and being a trusted mediator, would see you excel in a human resources department.

Driven by an obsession with fairness, becoming a lawyer would channel your Libra wish for justice. Your natural charisma and charm would be helpful in gaining clients' trust and your Air sign talent for communication would help you make an impact in the courtroom.

BALANCING AT THE TOP

You're a very friendly, sociable boss, not altogether comfortable being the one making all the difficult decisions. You can labour over the smallest choices, but when you make your judgement, your opinion is usually nuanced and well-respected. You make it very easy for your co-workers to communicate with you, and honest communication is heartily encouraged. Though it can sometimes be hard for you to draw the line between what's popular, and what actually works, your style is very open because you wish for everyone to see that you are doing your utmost to make things work. This approach can sometimes be very time consuming as you have to wait for democratic agreement and compromise, but you wouldn't be convinced of the ethics of anything too dictatorial.

Your clever charm means you can turn someone down for a pay rise but have them leave your office feeling better about themselves than when they went in. Less charitable colleagues may say your friendliness can get in the way of your work, but the opposite is usually true. When you need something done, people around you are happy to help, as they'll be keen to repay past favours.

Most compatible colleagues

Taurus – you're both Venus-ruled and understand that paying for a bon vivant lifestyle, requires diligence and determination.

Aries – you have an understanding that you're happy to do all the good-cop charming stuff, as long as they can take care of the shouty, bossy bits.

Libra – this is a great working relationship because you're on the same level, so when one of you is down, the other balances you back up again.

Least compatible colleagues

Scorpio – Scorpio can be something of a closed book at work, so you're never really sure where you stand or what their opinions are.

Aquarius – you have great fun together but when you need Aquarius to respect your authority they might behave like a sulky teenager.

Capricorn – Capricorns are suspicious of charming, people-pleasers and you're suspicious of sceptical lugubrious types.

Perfect
Libra Careers

Web designer

Relationship counsellor

Fashion designer

Human resources

Public relations consultant

Hairdresser

Event planner

Make-up artist

Art dealer

Lawyer

Libra
Work Motto

DIPLOMACY
IS THE ART
OF LETTING
SOMEONE ELSE
HAVE YOUR WAY.

Libra friends and family

*Y*ou're a dedicated people person and making friends is one of your most appealing talents. It's an area where your confidence shines, and you remember little details about new people that makes them feel included and special. Your interest in others is sincere and is the reason you'll have such a large pool of loyal pals from all walks of life. With a natural ability to ask the right questions, make them laugh and bring them out of their shell, even your most introverted friends bend to your charming insistence that they spend time with you.

Clued up on what's trendy, fun or interesting, you know the best places to be seen and will thoroughly enjoy a night on the town. The ritual of getting ready for a glamorous occasion with your buddies is something of a Libra speciality. Both sexes turn the preamble to going out into an art form, with music, cocktails and a thousand wardrobe changes. For a more low-key affair, you're happy to make your pals feel comfortable in your own home. You're a generous and thoughtful host, and will set up sophisticated cocktails, exceptional appetisers, and flattering lighting for a relaxing but elegant heart-to-heart.

FAMILY DYNAMICS

You view your home as an extension of your artistic talents, whether it's a bedsit or a swanky country house. Your taste is exquisite, and you'll have plenty of beautiful objects on display. Even more modest Libra homes will have a couple of designer pieces, elegant furniture or gorgeously sumptuous fabrics on show. Comfort is important but looking the part is essential! Your taste changes often and you regularly appraise whether your decor is reflecting your current tastes. Your restlessness and artistic standards can be a little frustrating for others but living with you is usually so pleasant that your partner, housemates or family tolerate your constantly evolving ideas of what looks good.

As the sign of relationship, you'll likely be keen to start a family, though, because you're so enamoured with romance, you'll be keen to keep your love story glowing throughout parenthood.

Your home must be tranquil, as you expect everyone in it to be as sensitive to bad atmospheres as you are. You like to remind the people who share your space how special they are and will have plenty of photographs of loved ones dotted around. Always balancing extremes, if your home or family life becomes too complacent, you'll announce a surprising trip or treat for everyone. And if things become too chaotic, you'll be the peacemaker calming everyone down.

LIBRA PARENT

Disliking authoritarian rules yourself, you can be a laidback parent who wants to be friends with your kids first and foremost. You tend to leave difficult conversations to the other adults and concentrate on being a loveable, fun, pal. This can sometimes mean you create blurred boundaries, which can be confusing for you all. Best to stick to a 'firm but fair' policy, where you all know what's expected from each other.

LIBRA CHILD

Emotionally intelligent and sensitive to negativity, little Libra senses when their parents are upset, which can cause them to get clingy. It's tricky for mini Libra to understand that saying 'no' to them doesn't mean they're not loved. Helping your Libra kids understand that their intense or difficult emotions are healthy will be both challenging and very rewarding.

Healthy Libra

*Y*ou love to look hot, Libra, and it can be a challenge for you to balance your love of food and a full social life, with a limiting diet or rigorous exercise plan. Venus-ruled signs are usually well-groomed and spend a great deal of care on their appearance, so getting hot, sweaty and breathless won't be your first choice when it comes to staying active. Ugliness disturbs you, and you can be harsh on yourself if you catch an unflattering glimpse of your puffy, straining face in a mirror. If you wish to feel balanced and happy, you will want to feel that you're not depriving yourself – after all is life really worth living if there are no champagne cocktails or chocolate truffles?

FOOD AND DRINK

Venus is a planet of enjoyment, and food will be high on your agenda. Venus-ruled Taurus and Libra both have quite slow metabolisms and are prone to gaining weight. Sweets, puddings and carbs are one of your greatest pleasures, but obviously there is a downside to all those delicious treats. Your busy social schedule means you're often at the mercy of other people's cooking, or exquisite menus in delightfully indulgent restaurants. It's hard to be disciplined when there's such an abundance of delicious goodies on show. Cakes, sweets and calorific bakery goods tend to be your favourite way to reward yourself, so you're unlikely to plump for a green salad when you're congratulating yourself on reaching a personal goal.

Balance is the key to your well-being, and your passion for indulgent food may be difficult to master, but there is a middle road. Air signs dislike feeling heavy after rich food, as it saps your vitality and makes you feel lazy. You can address the sluggishness by eating smaller, portions and keeping your food choices interesting. Or perhaps when you are at home, you can decide to prepare healthier but tasty options for yourself, but choose whatever you fancy from the menu when you're out for dinner.

ACTIVITIES AND RELAXATION

The gym doesn't hold much appeal – unless it's a cool place to hang out, in which case you'll enjoy spending time in the cafe, chatting to friends and blowing your hard-earned calories over lunch. If you do venture onto some machines, you'll be wearing the latest kit and will sneak a good look at what other people are wearing, too. As the sign of relationships, you prefer to work out with other people, so having a personal trainer or working out alone isn't for you. Tennis and squash, or any sports or activity requiring a partner, will suit your need to work with someone else, so ballroom dancing, Zumba, and water-aerobic classes appeal too.

To relax and unwind, talking with friends is your preferred way to chill. Talking out any problems and knowing that someone else understands where you're coming from is the best therapy. Counselling can also work brilliantly for you if you wish to express what's on your mind directly, without worrying about offending anyone or being too polite about how you really feel.

BODY AREA: LOWER BACK

Psychologically speaking Libra is associated with remaining in one position while balancing your thoughts and emotions. This restless swaying can result in an achy back as a consequence of sitting in the one place for too long and constantly having to adjust your position. Yoga would be a useful practice to help restore your sense of balance physically and mentally.

Libra on the move

*H*appiest in buzzing towns and cities with plenty of exciting action on the arts scene, you fit in easily anywhere with a fashionable, cultural vibe. Deciding where to go is the hardest decision – a beautiful tropical getaway somewhere remote and romantic? Or a frenzied shopping spree in New York? You first create a list of your favourite destinations *then* you look at your bank balance and credit card statements. A weekend at the seaside might not be right at the top of your list but even on a shoestring budget you'll be determined to visit the most exciting places on offer.

Holidays, road-trips, and fun experiences are all opportunities to indulge in the good life, and your Venusian penchant for splashing the cash needs to be tamed if you don't want to live the rest of the year on baked beans and toast.

SHARED EXPERIENCES

You rarely travel alone, preferring the company of a friend, partner or family. When you do go somewhere by yourself and discover something wonderful, it won't feel right that you can't share it with someone else. For you, life's most beautiful moments are only half as good if someone you care about isn't there to experience them with you. Travelling to a beautiful location with the person of your dreams is a Libra fantasy, so if you get the chance to whizz your loved one off to an exotic location, it will be something you'll probably remember forever.

If a romantic trip is not on the cards, then travelling with family or friends will prove just as interesting. You will enjoy spending your downtime with loved ones, catching up, strengthening your relationships and endlessly chatting about what's on your travel agenda.

You are quite seduced by social media's charms and, as you're all about projecting the right image, can't miss out on the chance to feel more connected to people. You often post pictures of yourself at the most captivating places, even if you know the enjoyment you feel is only on a superficial level.

VENUSIAN RAZZLE DAZZLE

You're not the most practical person when it comes to packing your bags and you'll scrimp on the practicalities if it means extra room for perfume, aftershave, expensive body lotions and hair treatments. You'll be hoping to be seen at your most glamorous, so your fabulous designer clothes take precedence over walking shoes.

You are the social butterfly of the zodiac, wanting to visit and be seen at the most prestigious events or the world's most dazzling locations.

You love dressing for a glam night on the town

and nightclubbing with the beautiful people in a sophisticated spot meets all your Venus, luxury-loving requirements. As you're also an intellectual Air sign, you'll also enjoy cultural events and festivals, lectures, book shows and vintage clothes fairs.

Wherever you decide you're going, when you get there you want the most luxurious options you can afford. That may be an extravagant hotel room with a sea view and fine Egyptian cotton sheets or glamping at a music festival, but if there's a more comfortable or opulent way to enjoy your stay – you'll take it!

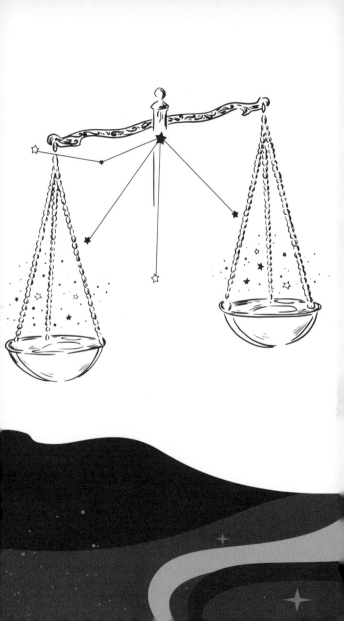

Libra
Favourite Places

Paris

Seychelles

Miami

Beverly Hills

Gstaad

Swanky nightclub

French Patisserie

Ibiza

Aurora spotting trip

St Barts

I'LL GO ANYWHERE,
JUST SO LONG AS
I'M GOING THERE
FIRST CLASS.

Libra
BIRTHDATE
PERSONALITIES

Discover your
personal forecast
for the day of
your birth.

24 September

*Y*ou are a self-sufficient and practical person with an artistic eye. Highly civilized, you are rational, articulate and graceful. You make a superb craftsperson as you have both artistic and technical skills. An attentive listener, you are a great manager as you are genuinely interested in serving people and would be well suited to the retail or restaurant trades. Your weakness is being finicky and over-analysing people and situations. However, when you let your hair down you have a whacky sense of humour. In a relationship you are an affectionate and devoted partner. You need to be able to share the same interests. You delight in domestic life and find joy in keeping the household running smoothly. Relaxing in a playful manner will balance you, so children's games are perfect.

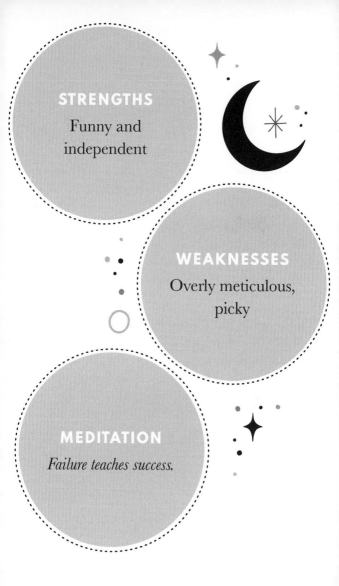

STRENGTHS
Funny and
independent

WEAKNESSES
Overly meticulous,
picky

MEDITATION
Failure teaches success.

25 September

*Y*ou are a beautiful and loving person with immense charm. The epitome of gracefulness and elegance, you are able to blend into any social situation with ease. You adore being around people and have a wide social circle. Whether professional, personal or family, relationships play a vital part in your life and you rely on them to help you understand who you are. This makes you very dependent on others for your well-being and you can be thrown off centre if you think someone doesn't like you. As a people person Public Relations would be an obvious choice of profession, as would a musical, modelling or acting career. In love you have a tendency to idealize your partner until you recognize they are only human. You can get lazy so exercise with a social aspect is an incentive – cricket or baseball fit the bill.

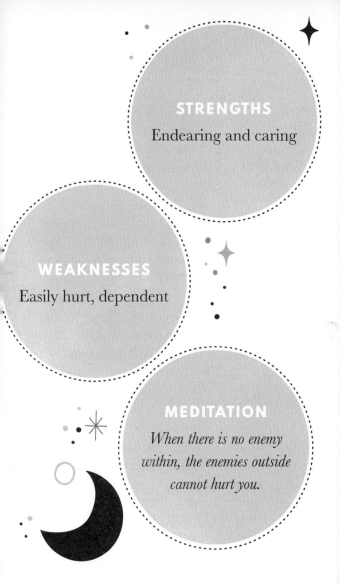

STRENGTHS
Endearing and caring

WEAKNESSES
Easily hurt, dependent

MEDITATION
When there is no enemy within, the enemies outside cannot hurt you.

26 September

You are a suave and magnetic person with great allure and mysticism. You can be mesmerizing to watch as you move with sensuality and grace. You have a combination of a sharp intellect and emotional strength, you are both charming and debonair so are popular with many people. Money and power are very attractive to you and a career in business or politics is likely. Show business is also appealing as you can handle the adulation and fame. With your courage and tenacity you can get to the very top of your profession. You are renowned for your willpower and can be a formidable enemy. If thwarted you can manipulate to get what you want. Your intimate relationships are intense and stormy as you relish drama. The opera or heavy rock music are your kind of relaxation because you love the passion in them.

STRENGTHS
Refined and
captivating

WEAKNESSES
Unscrupulous, overly
ostentatious at times

MEDITATION
*The real measure of
wealth: how much you'd be
worth if you lost all
your money.*

27 September

*Y*ou are an idealistic and persuasive person with a burning desire to share your vision with people. You believe in a better future for the world and that all people can have wonderful, loving relationships. With your flair and great organizational skills, you are the perfect campaigner for whichever pet cause you adopt. You are likely to be a spiritual person and have a missionary zeal that could take you into the ministry. You love to help people but you can overestimate your capabilities, taking on too many projects and thus spreading yourself too thin. You need a great deal of freedom in your intimate relationships so look for a partner who shares the same passion as you do for your projects. A weekend trip with your lover to explore a foreign culture would be an inspirational experience for you.

STRENGTHS

Great coordination
skills, obliging

WEAKNESSES

Over-stretching
yourself, prone to
burning out

MEDITATION

*Take rest; a field
that has rested gives
a bountiful crop.*

28 September

*Y*ou are a courteous and tactful person who is worldly-wise. Purposeful and ambitious, you can cultivate influential people to help you succeed. You enjoy being part of a team, have great organizational skills and make a superb manager. People respect your leadership and natural authority. You have impeccable taste and extremely high standards, which are exemplified by the designer-label clothes you wear. However, you can also have impossible expectations of people and need to learn to be more tolerant. To some you can appear snobbish, to others you are a steadfast friend. In your intimate relationships you need to be able to respect your partner and to feel adored. Physical affection is vitally important for you to open up your heart to another. Aromatherapy massage is a wonderful way for you to feel total relaxation.

STRENGTHS
Well-mannered
and enlightened

WEAKNESSES
Supercilious with
impossibly high
standards

MEDITATION
*We must never confuse
elegance with snobbery.*

29 September

*Y*ou are a freewheeling individual who seeks the ideal romantic relationship. Very friendly and sociable, you are a lively and witty companion. You adore discussing new ideas and solutions for the injustices in the world. With clear logic and a rational mind, you are a thinker and would be well suited to intellectual careers in technology and engineering. You want to know how things work and love solving problems. In your intimate relationships you can over-analyse as a defence against feeling your own deep emotions. You have impossibly high standards for how a partner should behave and are frequently disappointed. This keeps you independent and you can remain single for a long time. You need to discover a spiritual path which will fulfil you. Singing can help you open up and connect with your heart's desire.

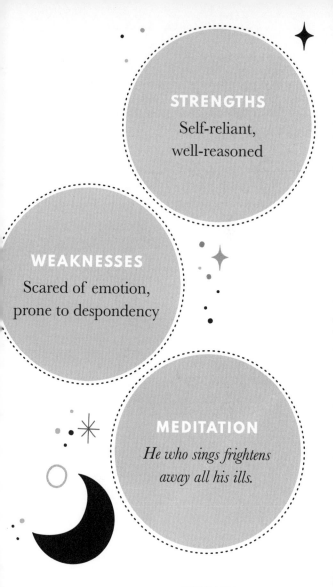

STRENGTHS
Self-reliant,
well-reasoned

WEAKNESSES
Scared of emotion,
prone to despondency

MEDITATION
*He who sings frightens
away all his ills.*

30 September

*Y*ou are a lively and intelligent person with a bright and breezy manner. You are ever-youthful and have a childlike innocence. Immensely curious, you are always asking questions, so you would be a natural journalist or writer. With a friendly style, you are skilled at putting people at their ease so they open up to you. Being an interviewer could be a rewarding profession. In relationships you get bored easily, always moving on to pastures new. Some say that you skim the surface and are afraid to go deep into your feelings, however, your significant other is very important to you, so slowing down to reflect on your emotional world helps you enormously. You are so easily distracted that giving your lover your undivided attention by turning off your gadgets, means more than words can say.

STRENGTHS
Inquisitive and
full of life

WEAKNESSES
Undemonstrative,
and at times, naive

MEDITATION
*Do not to stop questioning
– curiosity has its own
reason for existing.*

1 October

You are a convivial and lively person with a restless spirit who needs to experience new things on a regular basis. With high energy levels and plenty of drive and courage, you love taking the initiative and leading people. Your mind races ahead and you will try anything new. A natural champion of the underdog, you have a persuasive and direct style of talking which is hard to resist. As such, you are a skilled negotiator and would flourish as a diplomat. You are more sensitive than you appear and react badly to criticism, which can throw you off course. At times you make rash judgements. Love is what you live for, and all the rituals of courtship thrill you. However, you bore easily when the passion cools and will start a fight just to liven things up. Competitive sport is essential for you to let off steam.

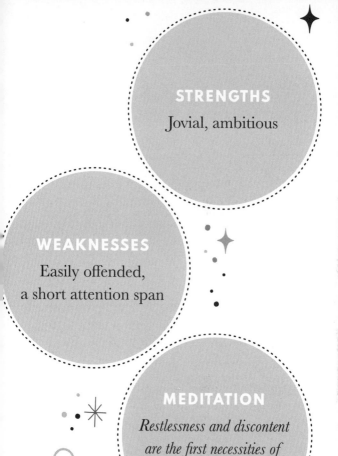

STRENGTHS

Jovial, ambitious

WEAKNESSES

Easily offended,
a short attention span

MEDITATION

*Restlessness and discontent
are the first necessities of
progress.*

2 October

*Y*ou are a charming and delightful person with a great sense of style. Very classy and with aesthetically good taste, you are one of the beautiful set. A lover of beauty and art, you are a creative and naturally drawn to work in the fashion or music business. You also possess good business acumen and can handle large amounts of money with ease. Relationships are essential for you and you are a keen lover. The problem is that you are extremely flirtatious and even if you do not mean anything by it, people are very attracted to you as you can make them feel special. You can also be tempted by a hedonistic lifestyle, which can cause your partner to be jealous. As a tactile and sensual person an aromatherapy massage is what you need, and what you can give to demonstrate your love.

STRENGTHS

Elegant and financially competent

WEAKNESSES

A thrill-seeker, coquettish

MEDITATION

Collect as precious pearls the words of the wise and virtuous.

3 October

*Y*ou are a sophisticated and engaging person with a lively wit. A gifted raconteur, you can charm almost everyone, but you can also be provocative and have a mischievous side to you. In a debate you love to take the opposite side just to stir things up. You manage to wriggle out of awkward situations through quick thinking and humour. The communications industry would be a good field for you, whether as a copywriter in advertising, or as a gossip columnist for a glossy magazine. At times you can be overly flippant and come across as emotionally immature. In relationships you need to keep it light and you can spend a long time playing the field before you settle down. Insomnia can be a problem as you are so mentally active – yoga in the evening and avoiding caffeine can help.

STRENGTHS
Droll, a raconteur

WEAKNESSES
Facetious, a tattler

MEDITATION
*There is a time
for many words,
and there is also a time
for sleep.*

4 October

*Y*ou are a warm and hospitable person with a caring, sensitive nature. A great friend and an excellent host, you love entertaining and making people feel welcome. The hotel and entertainment industries are areas in which you could excel. You have artistic gifts and need to express yourself in order to feel fulfilled. Your weakness is that you can be emotionally unstable and easily hurt by the slightest negative comment. A close support network of family and friends is essential for your confidence. An intimate relationship plays an important role on your life and it is rare for you to be on your own. Very affectionate, you need to be appreciated and respond quickly to a hug. You are naturally nostalgic and food is close to your heart, so a family picnic by the seaside makes a wonderfully soothing trip down memory lane.

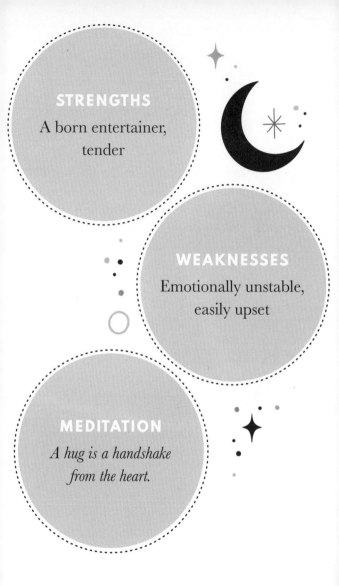

STRENGTHS
A born entertainer,
tender

WEAKNESSES
Emotionally unstable,
easily upset

MEDITATION
*A hug is a handshake
from the heart.*

5 October

*Y*ou are a vivacious, generous person with a warm and open heart. Your kindness and playfulness are very attractive and people love to be in your company. Leadership positions in the fields of politics, music or the theatre are appealing as career paths. You are self-confident and adore being the centre of attention. However, if people fail to recognize and appreciate your talents, you can get very upset and become quite temperamental. Your lifestyle is important and you often live beyond your means for the sake of keeping up appearances. Romance keeps your inspiration flowing and is an essential part of your life. The only problem is your tendency to worship your lover and keep them on a pedestal. Creativity is your strength so when your emotions overcome you, it's time to express yourself through your art.

STRENGTHS

Self-assured, with a sympathetic nature

WEAKNESSES

Highly-strung, and at times, needy

MEDITATION

Don't smother your loved one. No one can grow in the shade.

6 October

*Y*ou are an articulate and peace-loving person with fine reasoning abilities. You have a love of justice and are concerned with what people think. A natural advocate and campaigner, you are charming and diplomatic in what you say, nevertheless you can put your point across powerfully. You enjoy opening people's minds to new concepts, are patient and thorough, so make an excellent teacher. With your quick mind and cleverness you can appear to some to be aloof and cool. In your personal relationships you are faithful, devoted and enjoy the daily routines of family life. A problem of yours is that you can't bear mess, so can be obsessed with tidiness and cleanliness. You enjoy taking care of others and also need to be pampered. A day at a spa or on the golf course with a close friend would restore your equilibrium.

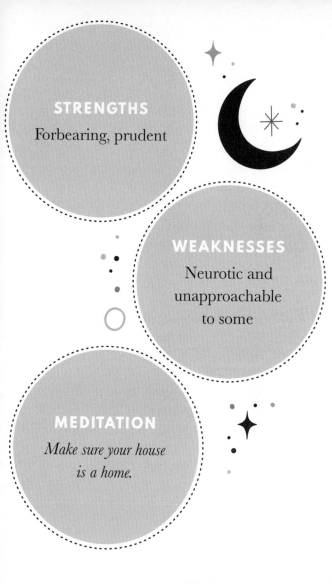

STRENGTHS
Forbearing, prudent

WEAKNESSES
Neurotic and
unapproachable
to some

MEDITATION
*Make sure your house
is a home.*

7 October

*Y*ou are an idealistic and refined person with a courteous and graceful manner. A born diplomat, your ability to put people at ease works well for you whatever career you follow. You are concerned with fairness and justice for all and are impartial and rational; so careers as a judge, lawyer or negotiator are all suitable. A lover of peace, you are also more than happy to fight for what you believe in and can be disarmingly outspoken. However, you express yourself with such impish charm that most people warm to you. Narcissism can be a problem as you are overly concerned with your appearance and are always stylish. Relationships are vital as you feel incomplete without a partner. You adore romance and a sport which is glamorous that involves your partner – such as skiing – is ideal for you.

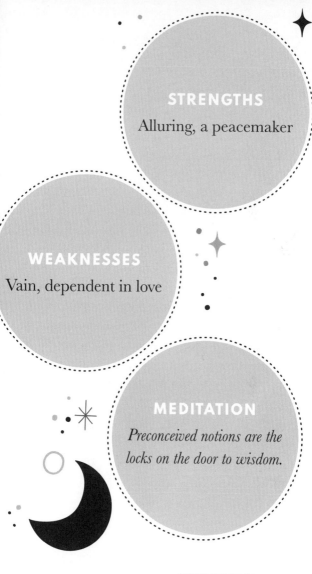

STRENGTHS
Alluring, a peacemaker

WEAKNESSES
Vain, dependent in love

MEDITATION
Preconceived notions are the locks on the door to wisdom.

8 October

*Y*ou are an astute and self-possessed person with good instincts. You can weigh people up and are an excellent judge of character and situations. Although you promote peace and harmony you are not afraid of conflict and can provoke a fight as you enjoy the intense emotions involved. Debating is one of your skills and you will gladly support the underdog. Politics is a natural arena for your talents, as is the law – you are incredibly effective as your enthusiasm and positive approach disarms any opposition. In your personal relationships you need depth – a light-hearted affair will bore you. Once committed, you can develop into a faithful and passionate lover, as long as your partner retains an air of mystery. Your weakness is that you can be insecure and suspicious. You need to express your raw emotions so martial arts appeal.

STRENGTHS
Wholehearted, fervent

WEAKNESSES
Self-conscious,
untrusting

MEDITATION
*Worry about what you
think of others and not what
they think of you.*

9 October

*Y*ou are a witty, humourous person, with a lively, original mind. You are diplomatic and unafraid of expressing the truth with compelling charm. You have strong convictions and are incredibly enthusiastic and vocal about your beliefs. People listen and take note as you speak from your heart. You would make an inspiring teacher, lecturer or educationalist as you truly desire to help and motivate others. A weakness is that you can appear proud and aloof and turn to work to hide from your personal problems. An intimate relationship supports your emotional growth if you can commit yourself and not get side-tracked by work and your many projects. Being spontaneous with your lover and suggesting a romantic weekend away somewhere warm and exotic can reignite your passion and give you the adventure you adore.

STRENGTHS
Adventure-seeker,
waggish

WEAKNESSES
Unable to relax and, at
times, unforthcoming

MEDITATION
*One should count each day
a separate life.*

10 October

*Y*ou are sophisticated, sociable and skilled in many areas. You have the confidence of an older person even when young and people choose you as their protector and leader. You are sensitive to others and make friends for life. Totally responsible and with a reverence for hierarchy, you are well suited to a traditional career in a large corporation, easily working your way up to management level. You love justice and could train for the Bar as you have the discipline for lengthy study. Some people can feel you are too controlling and authoritarian, but those who know you find you a sympathetic and witty companion. In your love life you are a devoted partner once you feel you have met your intellectual equal. To relax you need fun and something that loosens you up – dancing is excellent for you.

STRENGTHS
Wise, admired

WEAKNESSES
Dominant and
over-bearing

MEDITATION
*They that will not reflect
are ruined people.*

11 October

*Y*ou are a creative thinker with innovative ideas and a gift of clarity to disseminate them. Your diplomatic skills, combined with a social conscience and a desire to be truly helpful to your fellow man, would make you a gifted reformer or politician. Plus your persuasive logic and impartiality are assets for a brilliant negotiator. At times you can be impractical and live in your head, dreaming your life away. Your love life can be up and down as you yearn for the ideal relationship. You hold a vision of utopia and can feel extreme discomfort in dealing with deep emotions such as hate and jealousy. A good friendship can compensate for lack of intimacy and is a priority with your lover. You would come into your own at a debating society and a cocktail party gives you a buzz.

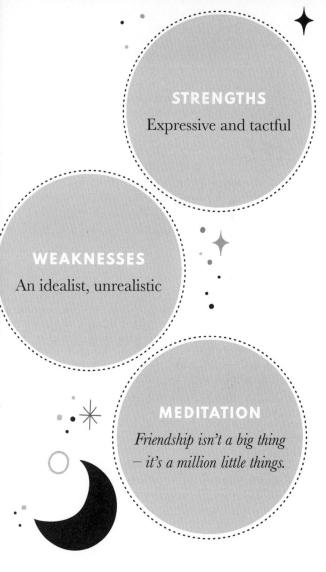

STRENGTHS
Expressive and tactful

WEAKNESSES
An idealist, unrealistic

MEDITATION
Friendship isn't a big thing – it's a million little things.

12 October

*Y*ou are a gentle and sensitive person who is a romantic dreamer. With your almost childlike innocence you can be endearingly sweet. You are very versatile and can easily adapt to situations. Artistic, musical and good with words, you inspire others with your vision of transcendent beauty. Your ability to understand and feel what others feel makes you a superb counsellor and group facilitator. A big weakness is in romance. You long for the ideal lover and have huge expectations which are impossible for a mere mortal to fulfil. Despite this, in your desire to keep a mate you have a tendency to become a doormat. Expressing your creativity is essential for you to feel valued. You enjoy relaxing with close friends and being by the sea touches your soul, so sailing can bring you deep contentment.

STRENGTHS
Likeable, compassionate

WEAKNESSES
Unrealistic, a walkover

MEDITATION
The cure for anything is salt water – sweat, tears, or the sea.

13 October

*Y*ou are an adaptable and ambitious person with a shrewd mind. You are both logical and sentimental, a fascinating and sometimes difficult combination. In your career you aim high and use your natural intuition with great aplomb. You have a natural empathy and people respond positively to you, as they feel that you understand them. Your family life is of equal importance and it is only when you create your own nest that you feel supported and secure. Managing people is a talent of yours and this can be used in business or politics. A weakness is your moodiness which leads you to withdraw and brood. An intimate relationship is essential and you tend to marry young. Cooking for a dinner party of close friends is your idea of a treat as you truly enjoy making people happy.

STRENGTHS

Determined and
kindhearted

WEAKNESSES

Capricious, a sulker

MEDITATION

*The real leader has no need
to lead – they are content to
point the way.*

14 October

You are a flamboyant and romantic person with great style and finesse. A quick wit, great sense of humour and sophistication make you an accomplished socialite. You enjoy being in the centre of the action and give of your best in a leadership position. Fashion and the media are just two arenas for your talents, just as long as you are in the spotlight. Wounded pride is your weakness as you tend to wilt if people say anything that you perceive as criticism, however, you have resilience and bounce back quickly. In love you can idealize your partner and get very disappointed when you discover their flaws – remember that no one is perfect! You are romantic by nature so old-fashioned ballroom dancing where you can strut your stuff together with your loved one could be a great way to exercise.

STRENGTHS

Fashionable and a great people person

WEAKNESSES

Wishful-thinker, unable to take criticism

MEDITATION

Dancing is a short-cut to happiness.

15 October

*Y*ou are a kind and caring person with a fine intellect. You are immensely practical and interested in people's health and welfare. Incredibly patient, with the ability to attend to every detail, you are able to work through the nitty-gritty of any project. The health and healing professions appeal to you, especially alternative medicine. Your strength is your clever mind, but your weakness is a tendency to be over-critical and controlling of others. Learning to overlook people's little or unimportant mistakes will increase your popularity. In love you relax and a committed relationship brings you the deep peace you yearn for. You need to be able to share your hobbies and artistic interests with your partner. Time spent detoxing and relaxing in a sauna or steam room together is wonderful for you both.

STRENGTHS
Solicitous, intelligent

WEAKNESSES
Fault-finding, forceful

MEDITATION
We are all full of errors,
let us mutually pardon each
other our follies.

16 October

*Y*ou are an elegant and cultured person who is charm personified. You have a strong sense of chivalry and are incredibly romantic. People see you as their knight in shining armour – whatever your sex. You will wage war on what you view as injustices and yet you are a lover of peace. Artistically gifted, you are a musician, artist, writer or actor – or maybe all of these. You abhor crudeness and vulgarity and your surroundings are harmonious and tasteful. Your worst trait is your indecisiveness and tendency to change your stance which can be very frustrating for others. You discover yourself through your intimate relationships, so your choice of partner is crucial. Once committed you are a gem of a lover. A competitive sport which involves your lover such as mixed doubles would be a wonderful way to add spark to your love life!

STRENGTHS
Ravishing and
artistically gifted

WEAKNESSES
Vague and indecisive

MEDITATION
Good decisions come from
experience, and experience
comes from bad decisions.

17 October

You are a hypnotic and sensual person with a powerful intellect. You love the good life and have an appetite for comfort and luxury. Your career has to challenge you and stimulate your strong intellect. Acting and the music business both fit this description. You are frank and honest in your dealings and can spot hypocrisy in people. You like to be in a position of power and cannot bear to take second place. You revel in deep emotions so need a relationship to fulfil your high standards and keep you intrigued. You can, however, be very moody and jealous, and need a lot of physical affection to feel loved. If your partner takes you for granted you are capable of having an affair just to get their attention. Deep tissue massage is excellent for soothing your body and easing your mind.

STRENGTHS
Outspoken and sultry

WEAKNESSES
Impossible standards,
distrustful in love

MEDITATION
*The only way to make
someone trustworthy is to
trust them.*

18 October

*Y*ou are an adventurous person with amazing energy and passion. You have strong convictions and high morals and will express your opinions on a wide variety of topics to anyone who'll listen. Your enthusiasm, combined with your attractive and congenial manner, means that people respond favourably to you. You can charm the birds off the trees if you set your mind to it. You are naturally generous and, at times, over-extravagant in your desire to help people. Your popularity brings you a great deal of good fortune and once you gain wealth you are a born philanthropist. In your intimate relationships you need a warm and tender partner who inspires you and can keep up with your fast pace of living. Active sports which stretch and energize your body such as karate or ashtanga yoga are ideal.

STRENGTHS

A born benefactor,
ardent

WEAKNESSES

Dogmatic,
unable to relax

MEDITATION

*Someone who has attained
mastery of an art reveals it
in their every action.*

19 October

*Y*ou are a disciplined and self-assured person with a strong determination to succeed. A great planner, you make decisions based on rational logic. You have a love of beauty and a harmonious, well-designed environment is vital for your peace of mind. Recognition is important and you work hard to get the top job in business or the arts. Your material possessions represent your achievements and you will save up to buy the most expensive items. A loving relationship is the foundation of your life. However, you can be too controlling and rational when it comes to emotions and you need to accept that you cannot be in charge all the time. Although you adore being with your lover you need time alone, so an early morning walk when the world is still asleep is a great time for you to gather your thoughts for the day.

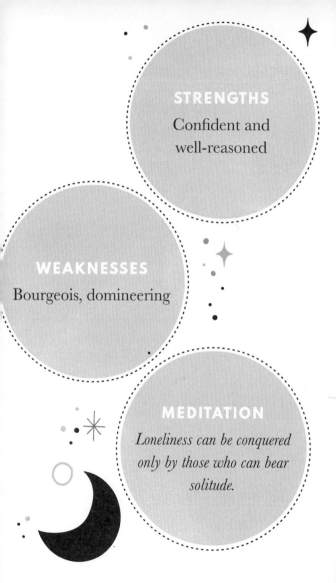

STRENGTHS

Confident and
well-reasoned

WEAKNESSES

Bourgeois, domineering

MEDITATION

*Loneliness can be conquered
only by those who can bear
solitude.*

20 October

*Y*ou are a likeable, attractive person who is very charming and easy-going, however, you do have a gullible side. You are a connoisseur of food, music and art and a sought-after member of many a social circle. People adore being in your company and want to please you. You need to live in a harmonious and beautiful environment, so a career in interior design is very appealing. You are sensitive to what people want and can interpret their ideas with flair and style. In your intimate relationships you are a wonderfully attentive lover and once committed, you are faithful. You can be too passive and if pushed too far will become stubborn to show your displeasure. Being out and about in nature is deeply relaxing and a sport – like golf – with its great social life has immense appeal for you.

STRENGTHS
Captivating, beautiful

WEAKNESSES
Overtrusting and
headstrong

MEDITATION
*Adopt the pace of nature:
her secret is patience.*

21 October

*Y*ou are an articulate and chatty person who is genuinely interested in what people think and feel. A keen observer, you know how to connect with and advise others, so work in retail or public relations is an excellent choice. You are constantly on the move and often on the phone. As an information junkie you love collecting details to pass on. Committing to one thing is extremely difficult for you and you can often break promises simply because you cannot say no to anyone. This carefree nature of yours is very appealing and attractive, however, in a long-term relationship your partner can find your excuses wear a bit thin. Learning about emotional intelligence will enable you to become happier. You benefit from an exercise such as tai chi or yoga which discipline and increase your mental focus.

STRENGTHS
Expressive and understanding

WEAKNESSES
Break promises, tendency to be unfaithful

MEDITATION
Learn to say 'no' to the good so you can say 'yes' to the best.

22 October

*Y*ou are an emotional and artistic person with a soft heart. The arts, history and culture all interest you and your career can follow many paths as long as you feel a strong connection with the group of people you work with. You are sensitive to the needs of others and care about the 'little things' that actually matter a great deal – you are the one who remembers birthdays and anniversaries. Your relationship is a priority in your life and you will settle down early. You adore domesticity and taking care of your family, but by being the nurturer you have a tendency to neglect your own needs. You are affected by negativity and can sense the mood of a room when you walk into it. Jacuzzis and steam baths are wonderful – as is swimming – for totally reenergizing you and lifting your mood.

STRENGTHS
Compassionate,
emotionally aware

WEAKNESSES
Prone to self-neglect,
feisty

MEDITATION
*Be positive — see the
invisible and achieve
the impossible.*

23 October

*Y*ou are a flamboyant and charismatic person with a huge appetite for life. In public you shine, you are a star and love to be in the limelight. However, in private you can be a recluse, preferring your own company or that of a few close and trusted friends. You constantly visualize yourself at the pinnacle of your career, as success is of utmost importance to you – you feel like an under-achiever until you're at the top of your profession. You can be ruthless in the pursuit of your goals and unaware of how you use others to get there. You have a strong sense of drama and are enamoured of the theatrical life. You need a relationship where you are adored, yet a partner who can gently remind you of the need to compromise. Organizing fund-raising events for a charity would be the ideal outlet for your passions.

STRENGTHS
Captivating, a born celebrity

WEAKNESSES
Hard-hearted, manipulative

MEDITATION
Never look down on anybody unless you're helping them up.

Going
DEEPER

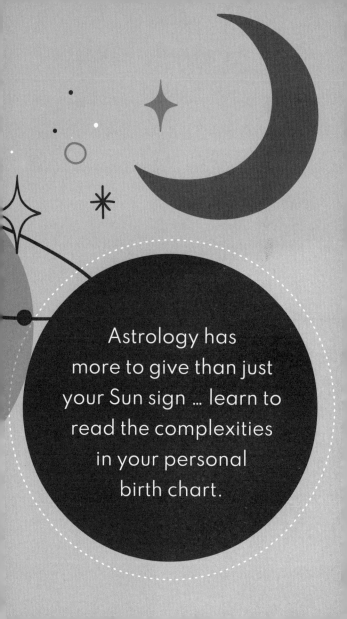

Astrology has more to give than just your Sun sign ... learn to read the complexities in your personal birth chart.

Your personal birth chart

*U*nderstanding your Sun sign is an essential part of astrology, but it's the tip of the iceberg. To take your astrological wisdom to the next level, you'll need a copy of your unique birth chart – a map of the heavens for the precise moment you were born. You can find your birth chart at the Free Horoscopes link at: www.astro.com.

ASTROLOGICAL SYNTHESIS

When you first explore your chart you'll find that as well as a Sun sign, you also have a Moon sign, plus a Mercury, Venus, Mars, Jupiter, Saturn, Neptune, Uranus and Pluto sign – and that they all mean something different. Then there are astrological houses to consider, ruling planets and Rising signs, aspects and element types – all of which you will learn more about in the birth chart section on pages 112–115.

The art to astrology is in synthesising all this intriguing information to paint a picture of someone's character, layer by layer. Now that you understand your Libra Sun personality better, it's time to go deeper, and to look at the next layer – your Moon sign. To find your own Moon sign go to pages 104–111.

THE MOON'S INFLUENCE

After the Sun, your Moon sign is the second biggest astrological influence in your birth chart. It describes your emotional nature – your feelings, instincts and moods and how you respond to different sorts of people and situations. By blending your outer, Libra Sun character with your inner, emotional, Moon sign, you'll get a much more balanced picture. If you don't feel that you're 100% Libra, your Moon sign will probably explain why!

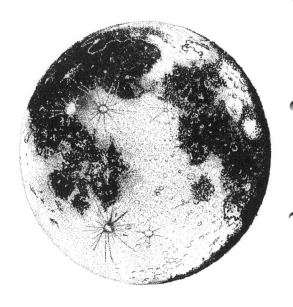

Libra with Moon signs

LIBRA SUN/**ARIES MOON**

Aries is your opposite sign of the zodiac, which means you are a full Moon baby. You embody some polarizing characteristics and may see-saw between two distinct sides of your personality. Your Libra Sun wants harmony and a balanced approach in all things while your Aries Moon is much more impulsive and decisive. Managing your mood swings is the key to your happiness and being able to take a step back to view whole situations rather than making choices based on one aspect that's affected you emotionally. You may also seek balance in how much of your time you want to spend on your own versus being in a relationship. You can become resentful if you don't have enough alone time, but you also want to share the good things in life with a partner.

LIBRA SUN/**TAURUS MOON**

This double Venus combination emphasises your love of the good life. You'll work very hard to be able to afford beautiful clothes and a swanky place to live but your indulgent, luxury-loving tastes can tip your scales into living beyond your means. Being tight with your purse strings will be challenging, especially as you are such a sociable person who likes to treat your friends. Your strong, practical and intellectual Earth/Air work ethic will pull you up by your bootstraps, and reign in any extravagant behaviour. You long for romance, but your choice has to be just right and you have the patience to wait years for the right person.

LIBRA SUN/**GEMINI MOON**

This double Air combination is a clever, adaptable and flexible mix and you're a witty, loquacious character. A little emotionally distant, you need to feel connected to your loved ones on an intellectual level. You look for a partner who is a friend first and foremost, someone who is as free-spirited as yourself. You are sociable and flirty and have a love of words, and a job where you write or speak all day would suit you well. You're a cultural dilettante who becomes obsessed with new ideas or people until you discover everything there is to know, then move on quickly to your next fascination. You will likely have a large group of acquaintances but you only let a handful of people get to know you on a deeper level.

LIBRA SUN/**CANCER MOON**

You're a philosophical, thoughtful and kind individual, who cares very deeply about your family and friends. You're empathic and diplomatic, with impeccable manners and a wonderful imagination. You can be easily hurt, but your Libra Sun is a good judge of character and helps you choose very trustworthy friends and a loyal partner. You're an exceptionally adaptable person who quickly absorbs different atmospheres, and you have a sixth sense in any social situation. You will avoid conflict and it may be difficult for you to stand up for yourself, but you have a charming and tenacious manner that usually allows you to get to the heart of any difficulties with others without getting annoyed or raising your voice.

LIBRA SUN/**LEO MOON**

You're a generous and sociable person, warm and energetic, happy to be at the centre of any gathering. You have an artistic outlook on life and will wish for beautiful surroundings. You have a touch of glamour and charisma and you don't settle for anything half-baked or below par. Your regal demeanour can sometimes fool people into thinking you're a little full of yourself, but you know that you need an audience to make you feel real and alive. Without others' encouragement and admiration, you can feel quite lonely, and working on your need for approval will be a useful endeavour. Idealistic and romantic your love life is never dull, though you need your partner's approval more than you care to admit.

LIBRA SUN/**VIRGO MOON**

Your Venus/Mercury combination helps you balance and reason your way through life. You're analytical, critical and observant, and your Venusian charm can sometimes beguile others into thinking you are all sweetness and light. Underneath your graceful, well-mannered personality is a razor-sharp intellect, and you'll require a stimulating or challenging job to keep your mind occupied. You demand very high standards from yourself, but your relationship-oriented Libra Sun prevents you from being too exacting of your friends and loved ones. Your work may be particularly important to you, and you may have to work through some challenges to balance your work and home life.

LIBRA SUN/**LIBRA MOON**

Born at a new Moon, you are a double Libra. You're an Airy Venusian through and through. You have impeccable manners and exquisite taste, and you shy away from conflict. It's important for you to stand by your opinions rather than be too influenced by what others think. It's tough for you to make decisions because you have such a nuanced sense of fairness that you wish to incorporate every viewpoint. You may need to be careful that your own opinion doesn't get lost in all the competing voices. Finding the right partner will be important, but your quest be may something of a learning process. You may meet many people who are relationship material – or very few – as you can't completely make up your mind what it is you want.

LIBRA SUN/**SCORPIO MOON**

 Your sharp Scorpio Moon gives you drive and determination, and you can be emotionally ardent and intense. On the outside you appear sociable, light-hearted and flexible, but inside you are deep, complicated and unfathomable. You are very seductive when you want to be, and people are attracted to your sociable yet slightly aloof personality. You are obsessed with justice and have strong opinions, and your passion and strength give you the will to succeed. You're a loyal partner but you need more alone time than most Libra Sun personalities. You find that you absorb other people's viewpoints quite easily and need time to work out which thoughts belong to others, and which are your own.

LIBRA SUN/**SAGITTARIUS MOON**

 This is an idealistic, optimistic combination. Your Libra Sun is outgoing, sociable and affectionate, and your Sagittarius Moon fuels your Air Sun with combustible Fire. You will be an adventurous, travel-loving person, restless and excited to experience all that life can throw at you. You are on a philosophical quest for truth and love a hearty intellectual debate. Your Libra Sun balances some of your over-enthusiasm with a more logical, detailed approach. You're probably a bit of a party animal and finding love will be a priority. You are a sunny-natured person and require a partner who is as open-minded and inquisitive as you are. You dislike being controlled or held back but also need someone to bounce ideas off before you make any broad-sweeping, impulsive decisions.

LIBRA SUN/**CAPRICORN MOON**

Your Saturn-ruled Moon allows you a more cautious approach to life than an out-and-out Libra. Capricorn Moon people are sensitive souls inclined to doubt themselves, but your outgoing Libra Sun will balance any gloomy tendencies and bring out your light-hearted side. You are talented and very ambitious, especially skilled in law or politics. Your diplomatic attitude and discerning judgment give you leadership qualities and you naturally know how to bring others together in business. You can be a little pedantic emotionally and trust has to be earned for Saturn-ruled Moons. But when you do place your faith in people you are earnest, loving and have a quirky sense of humour. You're actually a romantic at heart but would be the last to admit it!

LIBRA SUN/**AQUARIUS MOON**

As Libra is a sociable sign and Aquarius is passionate about improving society, working with groups of people will come naturally to you. Your philanthropic mindset means you may feel it's your duty to help others improve themselves and you may decide to teach or work with children. Friendship means the world to you, and you'll have many lifelong associations with people from all corners of the globe. Popular and cheerful, you dislike being on your own but aren't always looking for emotional support. You may wish to find a partner, but your Aquarian emotional detachment means you don't crave for another person to 'complete' you in the way other Librans may feel they do. Charming and self-sufficient, you have a quirky sense of humour and sometimes downright eccentric style – everyone knows who you are!

LIBRA SUN/**PISCES MOON**

You are a born romantic with an idealistic view of the world. A gentle, empathic soul, you feel other's pain all too easily. You're thoughtful and tender, always putting people first but should devote time to developing your own considerable skills. You may be drawn to write fiction, play an instrument or be an artist, as your imagination and intuition are very strong. You often make what should be logical decisions entirely on a hunch – and yet they usually turn out to be very successful. A kindly and flexible person, you make sacrifices to look out for everyone else, but shy away from working in your own projects and ideas. Finding a partner who can gently encourage your artistic talents would make you realise you have something special to offer.

Birth charts

*L*earning about your Sun and Moon sign opens the gateway into exploring your own birth chart. This snapshot of the skies at the moment of someone's birth is as complex and interesting as the person it represents. Astrologers the world over have been studying their own birth charts and those of people they know, their whole lives and still find something new in them every day. There are many schools of astrology and an inexhaustible list of tools and techniques, but here are the essentials to get you started ...

ZODIAC SIGNS AND PLANETS

These are the keywords for the 12 zodiac signs and the planets associated with them, known as ruling planets.

 ARIES
courageous, bold, aggressive, leading, impulsive

Ruling planet
 MARS
shows where you take action and how you channel your energy

♉ TAURUS
reliable, artistic, practical, stubborn, patient

Ruling planet
♀ VENUS
describes what you value and who and what you love

♊ GEMINI
clever, friendly, superficial, versatile

Ruling planet
☿ MERCURY
represents how your mind works and how you communicate

♋ CANCER
emotional, nurturing, defensive, sensitive

Ruling planet
☽ MOON
describes your emotional needs and how you wish to be nurtured

♌ LEO
confident, radiant, proud, vain, generous

Ruling planet
☉ SUN
your core personality and character

VIRGO
analytical, organised, meticulous, thrifty

 Ruling planet
MERCURY
co-ruler of Gemini and Virgo

 LIBRA
fair, indecisive, cooperative, diplomatic

 Ruling planet
VENUS
co-ruler of Taurus and Libra

 SCORPIO
regenerating, magnetic, obsessive, penetrating

 Ruling planet
PLUTO
deep transformation, endings and beginnings

 SAGITTARIUS
optimistic, visionary, expansive, blunt, generous

Ruling planet
JUPITER
travel, education and faith in a higher power

CAPRICORN
ambitious, responsible, cautious, conventional

Ruling planet
SATURN
your ambitions, work ethic and restrictions

AQUARIUS
unconventional, independent, erratic, unpredictable

Ruling planet
URANUS
where you rebel or innovate

PISCES
dreamy, chaotic, compassionate, imaginative, idealistic

Ruling planet
NEPTUNE
your unconscious, and where you let things go

The 12 houses

*B*irth charts are divided into 12 sections, known as houses, each relating to different areas of life as follows:

FIRST HOUSE

associated with *Aries*

Identity – how you appear to others and your initial response to challenges

SECOND HOUSE

associated with *Taurus*

How you make and spend money, your talents, skills and how you value yourself

THIRD HOUSE

associated with *Gemini*

Siblings, neighbours, communication and short distance travel

FOURTH HOUSE

associated with *Cancer*

Home, family, your mother, roots and the past

FIFTH HOUSE

associated with *Leo*

Love affairs, romance, creativity, gambling and children

SIXTH HOUSE

associated with *Virgo*

Health, routines, organisation and pets

EIGHTH HOUSE

associated with *Scorpio*

Sex, death, transformation, wills and money you share with another

SEVENTH HOUSE

associated with *Libra*

Relationships, partnerships, others and enemies

NINTH HOUSE

associated with *Sagittarius*

Travel, education, religious beliefs, faith and generosity

TENTH HOUSE

associated with *Capricorn*

Career, father, ambitions, worldly success

ELEVENTH HOUSE

associated with *Aquarius*

Friends, groups, ideals and social or political movements

TWELFTH HOUSE

associated with *Pisces*

Spirituality, the unconscious mind, dreams and karma

THE ELEMENTS

Each zodiac sign belongs to one of the four elements – Earth, Air, Fire and Water – and these share similar characteristics, as listed below.

EARTH

Taurus, Virgo, Capricorn

Earth signs are practical, trustworthy, thorough and logical.

AIR

Gemini, Libra, Aquarius

Air signs are clever, flighty, intellectual and charming.

FIRE

Aries, Leo, Sagittarius

Fire signs are active, creative, warm, spontaneous, innovators.

WATER

Cancer, Scorpio, Pisces

Water signs are sensitive, empathic, dramatic and caring.

PLANETARY ASPECTS

The aspects are geometric patterns formed by the planets and represent different types of energy. They are usually shown in two ways – in a separate grid or aspect grid and as the criss-crossing lines on the chart itself. There are oodles of different aspect patterns but to keep things simple we'll just be working with four: conjunctions, squares, oppositions and trines.

CONJUNCTION

0 degrees apart
intensifying

SQUARE

90 degrees apart
challenging

OPPOSITION

180 degrees apart
polarising

TRINE

120 degrees apart
harmonising

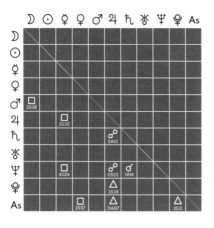

Planetary aspects for Amber's chart

HOUSES AND RISING SIGN

Each chart is a 360°circle, divided into 12 segments known as the houses (see pages 116–117 for house interpretations). The most important point in a birth chart is known as the Rising sign, which shows the zodiac sign on the Eastern horizon for the moment you were born. This is usually marked as ASC or AS on the chart drawing. This is the position from where the other houses and zodiac signs are drawn in a counter-clockwise direction. The Rising sign is always on the dividing line of the first house – the house associated with the self, how you appear to others, and the lens through which you view the world.

CHART RULER: The planetary ruler of a person's Rising zodiac sign is always a key player in unlocking a birth chart and obtaining a deeper understanding of it.

A SIMPLE BIRTH CHART INTERPRETATION FOR A LIBRA SUN PERSON

BIRTH CHART FOR AMBER, BORN 21 OCTOBER 1989 IN SYDNEY, AUSTRALIA AT 2.26PM

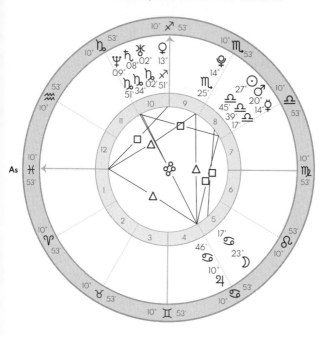

THE POSITIONS OF THE PLANETS: Amber has Pisces Rising. You can see that her Sun, Mars and Mercury are all in Libra, the Moon is in Cancer, Venus is in Sagittarius, Jupiter is in Cancer. Saturn, Uranus and Neptune occupy Capricorn and Pluto sits in Scorpio.

INTERPRETATION BASICS

As well as noting which signs the planets are in, you should also notice which houses they are in. How do you begin to put all these signs and symbols together? It's usually best to begin with the Sun and Rising sign (marked As on the chart), and then to examine the condition of the Moon sign.

SUN, MOON, RISING SIGN AND CHART RULER: Amber's eighth house Libra Sun is conjunct her Mars and Mercury, and all three planets form a 'stellium' which occurs when three or more planets sit together in a chart. Stelliums work as triple conjunctions, strengthening and highlighting the characteristics of the sign and its house position. Ruled by intense, deep, Pluto, the eighth house covers mysterious aspects of life such as death, surgery, regrowth and sexual themes. It's also a financial house, describing inheritances and money held jointly with others. Combine the eighth house symbolism with the driving force of Amber's personality (Sun), intellect (Mercury) and action planet Mars all in relationship-oriented Libra, and we could say that Amber may have to work hard to rebalance (Libra) this overabundance (stellium) of powerful (eighth house) energy from tipping her scales!

Amber's Moon (emotions) is in sensitive, home-loving Cancer in the fifth house of joy and creativity. Emotionally Amber is a caring and protective person who may be a little shy at first. She may choose to express herself creatively (fifth house) through the arts.

Pisces is Amber's Rising sign (AS), and so her first instincts when meeting new people or situations is to feel her way emotionally, then to go with the flow. Her chart ruler is Neptune (Pisces's ruler) which is conjunct Saturn (structure) and Uranus (change) in another stellium pattern in her Capricorn tenth house (ambitions). This is a strong tenth house as Saturn is in his own sign (Capricorn) and they're both in the house they rule, too – the ambitious tenth. Amber's double stelliums in the houses of career (tenth) and the eighth (money/sex/endings/transformation) ought to lend her a tremendous sense of purpose and determination. One basic, interpretation might be to suggest that Amber's career has been funded or fuelled by others, and perhaps at some point she will wish to break free to pursue a different path, and her Capricorn/tenth shows steely determination to succeed.

By looking at just these few points you immediately learn that the Sun sign's personality traits alone, although a crucial area of the chart, are often just one part of a person's overall picture.

OTHER PLANETS: Amber's Venus (relationships/love) is in philosophical, cheerful Sagittarius in the tenth house, which should give her an infectious sense of humour and joie de vivre, which will help balance her intense concentration of planets. Jupiter (luck/expansion) is in Cancer (sensitive/protective) in Cancer's home of the fourth house (home/family) showing a blessed and enjoyable home or family life.

Amber's Pluto (transformation) is very positive too, as it occupies Scorpio, the sign it rules, and is in the ninth house of travel/fortune and broad-mindedness. This is a strong, positive force for Amber.

ADDING IN THE PLANETARY ASPECTS

Let's take a brief look at the strongest aspects – the ones with the most exact angles or 'orbs' to the planetary degrees (the numbers next to the planets).

MOON SQUARE MARS: Amber can find her emotions (Moon) a little difficult (square) to control and she may be quick tempered and impatient (Mars).

MERCURY SQUARE JUPITER AND NEPTUNE: Sometimes Amber has so many (Jupiter) ideas (Mercury) that she might get confused (Neptune) or not know where to start (square).

VENUS SQUARE RISING SIGN (AS): Venus (love/relationships) can create tension (square) when Amber first meets new people (Rising sign/AS) or deals with unfamiliar situations.

JUPITER OPPOSITE SATURN AND NEPTUNE TRINE PLUTO AND RISING SIGN (AS): When Amber wants to push ahead (Jupiter), she may encounter obstacles (square) that inhibit her ambitions (Saturn) or limit her ability to imagine better outcomes (Neptune). But as Jupiter also trines (harmony) her Pluto (transformation) and her Rising sign/AS (how she approaches the world) Amber transforms on a psychological level to power through any opposition to her plans.

PLUTO TRINE RISING SIGN (AS): When Amber takes control (Pluto) of new situations (Rising sign) she usually creates fortunate (trine) outcomes.

YOUR JOB AS AN ASTROLOGER

The interpretation above is simplified to help you understand some of the nuts and bolts of interpretation. There are almost as many techniques and tools for analysing birth charts as there are people! Remember when you're putting the whole thing together that astrology doesn't show negatives or positives. The planets represent potential and opportunities, rather than definitions set in stone. It's your job as an astrologer to use the planets' wisdom to blend and synthesise those energies to create the picture of a whole person.

Going deeper

To see your own birth chart visit: www.astro.com and click the Free Horoscopes link and then enter your birth information. If you don't know what time you were born, put in 12.00pm. Your Rising sign and the houses might not be right, but the planets will be in the correct zodiac signs and the aspects will be accurate.

Further reading and credits

WWW.ASTRO.COM

This amazing astrological resource is extremely popular with both experienced and beginner astrologers. It's free to sign up and obtain your birth chart and personalised daily horoscopes.

BOOKS

PARKER'S ASTROLOGY by Derek and Julia Parker (Dorling Kindersley)

THE LITTLE BOOK OF ASTROLOGY by Marion Williamson (Summersdale)

THE BIRTHDAY ORACLE by Pam Carruthers (Arcturus)

THE 12 HOUSES by Howard Sasportas (London School of Astrology)

THE ARKANA DICTIONARY OF ASTROLOGY by Fred Gettings (Penguin)

THE ROUND ART by AJ Mann (Paper Tiger)

THE LUMINARIES by Liz Greene (Weiser)

SUN SIGNS by Linda Goodman (Pan Macmillan)

Marion Williamson is a best-selling astrology author and editor. *The Little Book of Astrology* and *The Little Book of the Zodiac* (Summersdale 2018) consistently feature in Amazon's top 20 astrology books. These were written to encourage beginners to move past Sun signs and delve into what can be a lifetime's study. Marion has been writing about different areas of self-discovery for over 30 years. A former editor of *Prediction* magazine for ten years, Marion had astrology columns in *TVTimes*, *TVEasy*, *Practical Parenting*, *Essentials* and *Anglers Mail* for over ten years. Twitter: @_I_am_astrology

Pam Carruthers is a qualified professional Vedic and Western astrologer and student of *A Course in Miracles*. An experienced Life Coach and Trainer, Pam helps clients discover the hidden patterns that are holding them back in their lives. A consultation with her is a life-enhancing and healing experience. She facilitates a unique transformational workshop 'Healing your Birth Story' based on your birthchart. Based in the UK, Pam has an international clientele.

All images courtesy of Shutterstock and Freepik/Flaticon.com.